I0019745

Cyber Criminals: The t use to Crack the Financial Industry and your precious assets

By Andrew Klein

Contents

Introduction

Cybercrime is as common as the common cold. A quick survey among a random set of my friends revealed that 9 out of 10 of them had been infected with a virus, 7 out of 10 of them had information stolen, and 5 out of ten of them had their information sold to third parties. This may not be the national average or the global average, but it's close. The US national average is that one out of every two persons is hacked.

But being hacked is not the only thing you need to think about. Everyone is worried about getting hacked but they do not take simple steps to prevent it, like using a Virtual Private Network, for instance. It's not fool proof, by any means, but it is a start.

If you left that statement with the idea that there is something worse than getting hacked, you're right. There is. Getting a virus can be worse, especially if that virus is designed to steal your data – especially your passwords. It can even be bad if they manage to get it on your contact list and spread their malware to your unsuspecting friends.

Most people still think that getting a virus is just about pranking. It's not. It's big business. And it's not about getting as many viruses out there so that anti-virus developers can make money. Yeah, I've heard that one too. None of the above is even remotely true. Viruses are ways hackers use to get into your computer to do all kinds of things. Even if you have no data to steal, you still have a contact list they can get to and spread to your friends, one of whom may keep his passwords or financial credentials easily accessible.

They could also use your computer as a drone or a zombie, where they control what they need your computer to do while you go about surfing. One sure sign that there is a problem is that your computer just gets really slow, while they are using your computer to hack someone else or to use it as a bot for DDOS attacks.

There are so many ways they could get to you and get you. In many cases, they take your information and sell it to the guys who really do a bit of harm. There is credit card fraud, there are fake purchases and so many other things they could do that could affect you or your credit score for a long time to come.

So what is this book for? Well, this book is to reveal all the little things these guys can do to you and your computer. We are doing this with one aim, and that is so that you can take the necessary precautions in protecting yourself, your family and your finances.

What we are also going to do is show you what it looks like from the other side of the fence. When you see it from the other side, you get an idea of the mindset that it takes to be able to execute a hack. It is not always easy, but it is also not as hard as one would think.

Just keep in mind that you shouldn't be too trusting of web sites, emails and links that come your way especially the ones that come unsolicited. These are the points of entry that can damage your computer and your peace of mind.

Take particular note of the chapters that discuss the methods of safeguarding login credentials and the ability to become anonymous on the Internet. The world of cybercrime stretches a lot farther and dives a lot deeper than most people realize. Hopefully with the strategies you find in this book, you will be able to protect yourself effectively.

Chapter 1 The Extent of the Cyber World and Information Technology

The Internet, as it is typically known, has only been around for a quarter of a century – a mere 25 years and in that time it's usage has penetrated over 80% of the population in the United States. A whopping 320 million people out of a population of 360 million consume content using the Internet. Collectively, most of these people spent a total of 360 billion Dollars in 2016 and that number is only looking to increase from there on. Globally, retail spending via the Internet alone will surpass over 1.9 trillion Dollars.

There are numerous statistics and benchmarks that we can point at and get an understanding of the size of the Internet, and most of them are pretty impressive. But there is one number that is pretty serious - 1,000,000,000,000 – yes, that's one trillion (no typo here – that's one trillion, not a billion). One trillion dollars will be spent between 2017 and 2021 on cyber security. More on that later.

The Internet is divided into three functional areas: The regular web, the deep web, and the dark web.

You and I toddle around the regular web – and that is pretty large on it is own. In 2014 the regular web had just under 900 million websites. In 2017 that reached 1.2 billion websites and will undoubtedly continue to grow.

Surface Web

The Internet has not only grown in the number of websites that are a part of it and the number of users that use it, it has also evolved in how it is used. It has been a social tool where we are able to keep in touch with friends and family and make new relationships. This is the social side of the Internet. Then there is the commercial side of the Internet, where we are able to do our banking, interact with businesses and services. We are even able to shop online for almost anything. There is also the informational value of the internet where almost every sort of data and information is available.

The Internet also serves as a platform for communication. This is slightly different from the social aspect but nonetheless, communication is a large part of the Internet's function. The uses go on from there to include getting directions, to understanding local culture and used in a so many ways that it would be too extensive to cover in a book that is about cybercrime. The point that you want to take form this is that the Internet is such a large part of so many lives that not having it around would be unfathomable.

That's just the regular web which is sometimes called the Surface Web. One way you can think about it is that if search engines like Google, Yahoo, and Bing index it then it's part of the Surface Web. Search engines index pages based on the links that they crawl. The term 'crawl' just means that the search engines automatically visit these pages and sites based on their link and then indexes them.

Then there is the Deep Web, and something even more nefarious-sounding, the dark web.

Deep Web

You wouldn't be able to find anything that is on the deep web on any of the major search engines. This is primarily because the way the search engines are set up. Engines like Google go in search of registered web links that are part of the formal infrastructure of the web. They are usually the ,com, .us, .info, .org and so on. But the web is not about formal links and centralized servers. Anyone that has a server and attaches an IP address to it, becomes part of the web. I am writing this for you right now on a laptop but I have some simple software running in the background that makes this 2008 laptop into a simple server that serves up data to any visitor who has the IP address or the link to it. Like that there are thousands of servers that can hold information that does not need to be formally registered or have a formal link. Setting up servers is easy if you know how. You can have anything on them and you don't need someone like Google to index them if you already have a following or if you are not relying on people finding you on the net.

There are web pages that are behind the surface web that does not get indexed (indexed is the term that is used for pages that search engines keep on their record so that when you search for something that is related they give you the relevant site that you searched for. For instance, if you go to a particular website and instead of clicking on its links you used its search box (the one that is on the website) and that one gives you are results that are not linked anywhere else, then the chances are that that page is not indexed by the search engine. The same goes for your personal data pages where you are required to sign in before the page is served up.

So for instance, if you were to go to one of the major search engines and type a search for government grants, it would lead you to the grants home page. It will not, however, lead you to any specific grants. To get to those you have to search for it in the search box on the home page. This is the deep web.

To make it simple deep web pages are not indexed by search engines, and surface webs pages are index by search engines. There is nothing nefarious or illegal about them. There is nothing shady going on here for the most part. They are just not indexed. Just so you get an idea, the deep web is about 500 times the size of the surface web. SO if the surface web is currently at about 1.2 billion websites and each website averages 20 pages then the size of the deep web is about one trillion pages. That's about all you need to know about the deep web.

Dark Web

Then there is the Dark Web. The dark web is like the deep web in the fact that it does not have its links indexed by the major search engines. Instead, they use what is called harvest engines that keeps tracks of sites in the dark web.

To access these sites it is best that you enter thought eh use of a special browser and a special relay system.

The most popular of these relay systems is called the TOR network. TOR stands for The Onion Router. To takes your search or your links and routes it through a vast network of other computers so that when it gets to the destination server, the server only sees the last IP address that the query exited from. SO for instance if you have a chain of five IP addresses the TOR browser will go to the first, from there it will bounce to the second then the third and then the fourth and the fits before it moves to the intended page.

You do this so that if the site you are visiting is tracking you or trying to find out who you are, they would not be able to track you easily. Mind you, it is still possible to back track to you if the person is motivated enough. That is the reason you take other measures as well when visiting the Dark Web.

The point to note is that the web is a simple set of relationships. You enter the URL or the IP address and your web browser goes through the wires and searches out the server that are associated with that address. It finds out where the address is located by looking up the DNS record. Once it has the location it goes straight to the server and asks for the information that you clicked on or typed in.

IN the surface web, you can be certain that that web page that you're requesting is going to come back as a legitimate page and it's going to come back with data. In most cases, your browser is just going to take that data and populate your screen. But in the event that it has some form of malicious software, then you are not going to know about it unless you have some super fancy antivirus software running.

This is the reason you never visit sites that you don't trust. Some of the credible browsers also have the ability to tell you and warn you of the site you are visiting is infected, but the people who run these sights are extremely clever and to them, antivirus software is just a little bump in the road. Your antivirus software won't know you've been infected for weeks to come.

That's a fact that you need to remember. AV software has a limited defense in the face of truly smart malware. So protect yourself when you want to visit the dark web.

What's on the Dark Web?

This book is about cybercrime so the best place is to start with the dark web. Because this is where you can find most of the tools and services you would need to perpetrate any of the things that would fall into the category of cybercrime. On the dark net, you can find hackers, you can find software and you can even find data for sale. So if I wanted to hack into your home computer and had a little bit of information on you, I just would get to the dark web, find a hacker, give him your information and in a couple of days he would hand over to me a bunch of things about you that you wouldn't even know about.

There are two things that you should know about this. First, that any hacker could get information about you, and second because they are for sale, anyone can get information about you. This is just the beginning. Before we get deeper into how that works we will look at the structure of the cybercrime organizations in the next chapter.

Chapter 2 The Structure of Cyber Crime

Let's get some terms in order. First off, cybercrime refers to criminal acts perpetrated through the internet. That's a really wide area to cover. We will break it down for you and show you the layers that have become the most popular in the cyber criminal's world.

In the last chapter, we introduced the possibility of hiring a hacker and getting your data by giving him some initial information and paying him for his time. But there is a lot more to that than just targeted data. It is, of course, possible and prevalent, but that is not the full structure of cybercrime.

The first thing that you need to appreciate is that the total size of this industry is $1 trillion. Has that gotten your attention yet? Well, it should. Hacking is not about a kid in the basement or some hooded guy tapping away on an old laptop. Cybercrime is a major avenue of income for the world's criminal underground.

The dark web, and many parts of the deep and surface web form significant parts of the supply chain and the distribution channel for illegal products and services. How does this industry turnover a trillion dollars? Well, there are numerous criminal acts that they can perpetrate in the online world. From selling contraband to pornography to prostitution. There are even forged documents for sale, that go from simple fake ids to sophisticated passports. There are also hacker services that we talked about earlier. But more importantly, there are also viruses for sale and programs that can hijack your computer. But since this book is about financial hacking in the financial industry, we are just going to narrow down the scope of this chapter to the ways financial information is harvested and how you are the victim.

Bots

Let's start with the simpler of the many ways that you are vulnerable and probably complicit without even knowing it. Have you ever wondered why viruses exist? I asked that question once to a room full of people and the consensus was that viruses were developed by nerdy kids for antivirus companies so that the antivirus company could then sell you the software to stop your computer from freezing up or something like that.

That is an interesting perspective on it except it's not true. AV companies build antivirus software for legitimate reasons because there are viruses out there that can cause severe damage to your computer. There are some that are more malicious than they are criminal. Their entire purpose is to shut your computer down. There are even things called ransom ware this day where they look up your computer with a virus and you can't get any for your data from the hard drive, then they flash a message on your screen telling you that it's a virus and you should pay some amount of money to get the virus neutralized.

But all that aside, viruses that do widespread damage do so by infecting your computer and then wrest control of your computer to the person who infected your device. It is so sophisticated these days that you and your computer won't even know that you've been infected. No matter how religiously you scan your computer. The code they upload to your machine will probably go undetected.

Once they have their code in your machine, you become their bot. Your machine will now do what they ask it to do and do it with priority and without your knowledge. To most people, they have no idea. They just think that sometimes their computer gets slow on them for whatever reason. What they do not realize is that the computer's resources are busy doing their master's bidding.

Data

The other thing that they do to you is enter your computer and then start going through your files, your emails, and your passwords. They even have enough control to use your computer to get to your bank account and to see what's in it. They look for things like bank balances, credit card information and get to know your financial profile to the best of their ability. With today's world being almost totally digitized, they can get almost any information that they want to and you wouldn't' even realize it.

Organization Structure

There are our levels in the cybercriminal's loose organization. I say 'loose' because each level of the organization is independent of the other and don't necessarily need to work together or be loyal to each other. This is not a job where they get benefits and pension schemes. The highest layer of the organization is the Consumer. The consumer here is like the mastermind behind the monetizing portion of the activities. It is this layer where all the data that is stolen is monetized. You have to remember one thing. The crime that is committed here is not the modern day version of a highway or bank robbery. What is stolen is really just electronic data. So even after it is stolen, that data needs to be converted or it is of no use. The consumer deals with the Dealer. The dealer does the physical work of performing the attack. The Dealer gets the targets to attack from the Farmer, and the farmer gets the background information from the Researcher. Here is how all this works.

Researcher

Hackers start by going after vulnerabilities. These are weaknesses in the target computer. In some cases, it is the design flaw in the operating system. In other cases, it is the design flaw in the browser. Whichever point they are targeting the Researcher's job is to go after the various penetration opportunities. The

Researcher, however, does not actually do any hacking; they do a lot of penetration testing (pen-testing) and then they hand over their research to the next level in the organization.

Farmer

Farmers use the research collected by the Researcher and use that to build botnets. A bot net is just short for Robot Network. A botnet is but by creating a form of virus or an exploit. When the Researcher gives the list of vulnerabilities to the Farmer, the Farmer builds the explant to take advantage of the vulnerability. All he is doing is writing code, either written in C++ or Python and allow the program to take control of the computer that is ingested. It is, essentially, a virus that can be persistent and invisible. It is invisible from the antivirus software that the target has installed on the system and it is persistent even when the computer is shut down and restarted. The farmer has one objective here and that is to infect as many computers as possible and to be able to take control of them without their knowledge. The Farmer doesn't take any data or do anything other than infect and take control.

Dealer

This is where things get interesting. The dealer purchases or rents all the bots in the bot net. The bots are the individual computers in the network. There can be as few as a hundred to as many as tens of thousands of bots in one botnet. When the Dealer rents these bots he can now do with them as he pleases. In some cases, he uses them to conduct phishing attacks or even send spam. He may even combine it and send spam that is actually a phishing attack. Dealers also conduct brute force attacks on hard drives to extract password information or other kinds of financial data. Most of the time credit card data is the most valuable to take and is one of the most prevalent pieces of data that is taken.

Consumer

Finally, there is the mastermind of the operation that decides what to do with all this data. This is the strata where all the data that is stolen gets monetized. It is the Consumer who pays the Dealer, who then pays the Farmer who then pays the Researcher. This is the last step in the chain where all the hard work pays off. The consumer uses the stolen data to conduct financial transactions. For instance, if credit card data is stolen, fake credit cards are made with the data and those are there sold or used to purchase items that are then sold in the black market. They may also be used to create fraudulent transactions. Where the Consumer is actually the vendor who 'sells' the product and uses the cloned credit card to make the purchase.

This is the chain of professionals that are behind the financial cybercrimes that happen every day around the world These organizations do not have a structured office but they have structure and are highly organized.

A 2014 study placed the direct amount of loss due to cybercrime at about 500 billion Dollars. This is just the direct cost that we can gauge. There are other ancillary losses that are not included in this figure. It is not easy to put a face to cybercrime although the popular face that it carries now is the mask of Guy Fawkes.

More and more people are recruited into this industry in the hopes of being able to make a ton of money. But just like all criminal conspiracies and organizations, the lower levels of the pyramid share a small piece of the pie and face some of the greatest threats. The higher ups get to take a larger chunk of the profits and are pretty insulated from the authorities. Of course, there are times when they do get caught, but in most cases, the masterminds do not face many risks and so continue to expand their operations with impunity and greater profit potential.

The cybercriminals, especially the ones that engage in financial crimes use a number of methods to get to your information and its' not always about hacking your personal computer or your laptop. They have now also found methods to hack into off site banking databases and clouds servers to extract large volumes of data that they can use for their operations. We will visit this area in the next chapter.

Chapter 3 How You are Vulnerable to Cyber Theft

In the last chapter, we saw one side of the coin. We saw the organizational structure that was involved in targeting personal computers and getting control of them. In this chapter, we are going to expose the other side of the coin and see how cyber criminals steal data and exploit vulnerabilities from the main servers where your information and data is stored.

One of the more recent incidents that saw the expansion of the hacker's ability was the hacking of the SWIFT wire transfer system. The amount stolen was not large compared to what they are typically capable of, but what was worrisome was the fact that the world banking system was considered tamper proof and that SWIFT themselves were not the weak link in the system It turns out that the hackers were able to penetrate one of the banks in the network.

This should illustrate to you that it is not just your home computer that is at risk but there are tools that are available, quite easily in fact, that allows the hacker to engage and penetrate large corporate servers and secure internal servers.

To put the SWIFT incident into perspective, the one thing you need to realize is that even though the last heist was just over 80 million dollars, SWIFT conducts more than a trillion dollars in daily transactions. If they hackers could penetrate the systems effectively, any loss to occur in the future would be catastrophic.

How does this tie in with you? You are, after all not a bank. The way this ties into you is that your information and your cash is in the possession of the bank's servers. They can tap in and take out money from the SWIFT system, they can easily take out your data.

Take another incident for example - the adult dating site Ashley Madison. While no financial data was stolen here, the problem is that they hackers were able to pull up all the personal information that was kept on Ashley Madison's servers and exploited the data, using it to blackmail the members on an individual basis.

Most hacks happen on an impersonal level over a wide area of users. But it can also be that the hackers target you individually and purposefully. You have to be vigilant with all your data all the time because they can get in with the slightest crack. It's easy to say that hackers are unscrupulous or are evil. None of that helps in your defense against them. The person hacking you could very well be your neighbor or your kid's classmate. There is no way to know who it is and in the case of defending yourself from an unknown attacker means that you have to be as cold as they are in defending your own interests. No one, including simple AV programs, are going to be able to do it. As you progress through the book, I will show you some of the tips and tricks they use so that you can protect yourself from this attacks.

There are multiple points in the chain of Internet consumption that will lend itself to an attack. Here is a list that shows you the number of points that are vulnerable.

1. Mobile Devices
2. Desktop Computers
3. Wi-Fi Connections
4. Routers
5. Public Networks
6. Web Sites
7. Free Downloads
8. Links

9. Emails

10. Torrents

These ten items are not a specific category of threat, they are just all the points that an attacker could mount an assault.

Mobile Devices

Mobile devices present a recent problem. There are three routes to hack your mobile device. One of it is to enter through your devices text service. You may believe links that only require that you open them to be able to have the packet that follows them to be automatically installed into your device's operating system environment. From that point on the device is fully/partially controlled. If it is partially controlled, that would not last for long as once they get a foot hold, Farmers are able to exploit further and fully penetrate your system. Hackers get your number from other infected devices that they have penetrated, or when they hack servers that contain your phone number. So, for instance, if I manage to hack Verizon's database and pull customer data, there are a number of things I can get. First off, I can get the mobile number of millions of customers.

Second I can find the IMEI and hack the device directly or clone the device. I can even get the SIM information and redirect information to my device.

Desktops

Desktop assets are valuable because most people keep tremendous amounts of personal information and data on their desktops. Most of their data is wide open because they feel in their home environment more so than in the mobile environment. The desktop user feels safe because he feels he is in control of the data chain from the pole to the Wi-Fi transmitter in his home. However, hacking a desktop is fairly easy especially if there are some pieces of information that the hacker gets. Desktops are gathered via a couple of means. They can either be harvested using torrent sites (which is discussed later) or from infected websites. Desktops are particularly vulnerable to virus attacks and exploits because of the nature of the operating system. Most Windows based systems have vulnerabilities that are constantly exploited by hackers. Each time a vulnerability is found, the OS make will update the software. So if you are using Windows 10 for instance, and there is a vulnerability that they find out about that some hacker has exploited, Microsoft will create a fix for it and update your system. But you must know that this happens after someone' is infected and there is a chance that you are one of those people who are infected. To minimize this occurrence always keep your computer updates and do not visit sites that are shady.

Wi-Fi Connections

Wi-Fi hotspots in public areas and even Wi-Fi hotspots in your home are a significant weak link in the entire data chain. A hacker with a laptop in range of the Wi-Fi transmitter can wreak havoc on every person that is in the range of that Wi-Fi transmitter. There is something called the Man in The Middle Attacks and how this works is exactly how it sounds. They set up their computer in such a way that transmits the signals that they get from the Wi-Fi router. They do not even need your password but as long as you are transmitting and the computer thinks that you are the Wi-Fi hotspot it's going to transmit to you. They literally stand in the middle, take the signal you are transmitting and they retransmit it back to the Wi-Fi hotspot. Then the data goes on its way to the destination that you intended. When that destination returns data to you, it comes back through the Wi-Fi hotspot and goes to the hacker's computer first before then finally coming to you. The Wi-Fi hotspot transmitter thinks that the hacker is you and your computer thinks that the hacker is the Wi-Fi station. All the while this is happening, the hacker is processing the data that is going back and forth. If in that time you enter your credit card number and the CVV number that is the three digit number behind the card, or if you enter your PayPal credentials, then the hacker has got all that information. Typically if this is a lone hacker then he will penetrate your system. But most likely he will sell this to someone who can use it. One of the secrets (not so secret among hackers) is a software called Wireshark. It is used to sniff the network and sniff the data that is passing through the Wi-Fi hotspot. You don't even need to be a Man IN The Middle to do this, just as long as you can get access to the Wi-Fi hotspot. To be able to do the Man In The Middle, there is a software specifically for that and hackers, or anyone can download it for free.

Routers

In many cases, in the home, the routers and the Wi-Fi transmitters are collocated. Routers are just devices that act as an information junction. They take the information that is coming in and send it to the machine that is connected to the router where the data request came from. Routers are just as vulnerable as Wi-Fi hotspots and are also a weak link in the data chain. Routers are not as highly protected as machines and hackers can get to them easily just by scanning networks and looking for IP addresses and identifying what device it is by analyzing the operating system on the device. A point to note that there are numerous free tools out there that can be used to compromise routers. But the one that is most important is to be able to get the router is itself. T do that the software of chose that is free to download is a network scanner called NMAP. NMAP pings all the devices that are in a certain range of IP addresses that you specify and it then goes out and maps that entire range. The results will show you what is on that network, what OS is being used by which device. It then compares that to a data able and accurately pinpoints what router or what device it is. From there on all you have to do is look at the list of vulnerabilities that are specific to that device and use the exploits that you find in a database. There is even a tool for that, which is also free to download.

Public Networks

These are Wi-Fi networks like the ones you get at your local coffee shop. The reason these are vulnerable is that they do not offer any protection for those who are connected to them to get to the internet. However, they do have firewalls protecting their own devices. Hackers that are more surgical in their approach and not part of the larger hacker collective, use these public networks to latch on to devices that log into these public networks and then they use one of few different methods to plant a back door, or what is called a RAT. RATs are Remote Access Terminals. RATs just require a short piece of code to be placed in the device and from there on, hackers can take control of almost all areas of the device. They can even get a screen capture, download the contact list, read email and even access the IMEI or the SIM card number. If it is a device, being able to install a RAT is even simpler as even the youngest novice is able to download one of a number of RATS that can be modified to suit their purpose and then deploy it. If you are thinking that there must be antivirus software that is capable of blocking them or having firewalls that prevent them, well then you are partially right and almost half way tech savvy. That's because most people are too trusting with their devices and oblivious of the danger it poses to their data and their financial well-being.

Web Sites

When you visit a website you are freely inviting the website to send data to your computer. Most of the time it is harmless data that comes back to populate your browser that eventually allows you to consume the information and images on your screen. However, even the most innocuous website these days carries with it tracking data. That may seem harmless but that tracking data does a lot of the hacker. Inside the file of tracking data, there is a boat load of information that is being collected. Everything from where you are to what you are doing on the net and where you visit. One of the hacks that is especially vicious is what is called social engineering. It is one of the methods, not a tool, that hackers use. Social engineering is when the hacker specifically targets you and those like you with emails and scams that target you specifically, based on your habits. SO for instance when they hack a company's server and pull all the tracking data, they use that data in conjunction with the NMAP scan of your environment to be able to understand where you are, what device you use, how long you are online, when you are online, and what your online habits are. The most likely will have your email address as well. All they have to do is send you an email targeting your interest to perhaps give away something free. The moment you click on that link, the virus loads on to your device and they have you. IN the same way, if you visit a website that you are not familiar with and they entice you with all sorts of giveaways, the links that you click on will load scripts on to your computer and execute a program that gives the Researcher, and eventually the Dealer, access to your computer.

Free Downloads

Free downloads are vicious. Hackers set up these sights that give away lots of stuff that people are looking to get for free. The best ones are movie download sites or other free giveaways like expensive software. The point is that the weakest link in any system is the human consumer. The weakest link is what hacker is good at exploiting, characterized especially by the ingenuity and creativity of some of the phishing attacks that they use or the social engineering strategies that are deployed. Never take on a free download, or if you have to check the download link with Virustotal. Virustotal is a free service where you paste the link of the item you wish to download and they will download the item and scan it. They also have a record of how often that link was scanned and what the past results were. They use a large number of tools to scan the link, not just one or two AV programs. SO the results that they give you are pretty close to accurate. However, you must remember that viruses that are new or not detected will not be in any antivirus definition file. They may be able to pick up traces or patterns, but that is not to be relied upon.

Links

There are a number of things that hackers can do with links. We have talked about some of these things under other headings. But the one that is most relevant to links is that they can read one thing but direct you to somewhere completely different. This is called link spoofing and you can do it to a point where it is completely undetectable. For instance, you could compose a link that reads https://www.xyzbank.com/login That link looks like the regular login that you would go to log into your bank account. But the spoofing that they do allows that URL to show up on the address bar and in the bottom corner of your browser, but when you click on it, it will take you to some server somewhere that can load virus on to your computer or prompt you for your user id and password like you will see in the next section. Links should never be clicked on but hackers know that most of us are quite lazy when it comes to the internet and we believe what we see. Combine the two aspects of human behavior and hackers know that the weakest link in any data theft operation is the human being. Porn sites, torrent sites and anything sounding too good to be true as probably something hiding in those links that you wouldn't guess. There are even lesser ways that hackers get surfers to click on links and that is by placing a link without even placing the URL. Links with terms like "Click here" or something like that usually proves sufficient to get people to click and get infected.

Emails

The best place to start is as simple as having an email address. Email addresses can be obtained freely from anywhere. Most hacker forums have dumped emails (email lists that contain data hacked from a database) which you can freely download. If you want databases of emails that are fairly new and haven't been spread around then some lists can cost you a couple of hundred bucks. Once you have these lists, it usually comes with passwords as well.

Hackers do one of two things with this list. They either try to gain direct access to your email account where they can get a wealth of information. The simplest trick hackers use when they get your user id and password for your email is that they try that combination with PayPal, and other financial sites. It doesn't take them long to hit the major ones and if you use the same user id and password as your email, then they are going to get access to your financial assets.

One of the best social engineering tools that are available, for free I must add, is called BeEF. It is the acronym for Browser Exploitation Framework. BeEF allows a hacker to do two things at one go. First, they can clone any website. Let's say they have detected from your browsing history that they obtained from the cookies you allowed for another site, that you typically bank at XYZ Bank.

They know that you typically go to the bank's website and input your credentials and conduct your banking activities online like pay for stuff or transfer cash to your ATM account. Hackers then go to the bank's web page, and at the click of a button can copy and clone that page. The result is an identical copy of the site. They then host that site remotes on any server they like and it doesn't even need to be a server that is paid for. They could host it on their laptop like I mentioned earlier.

They then send you an email that says that there is a discrepancy with your account and that you need to go into the account and sort it out. They conveniently place a link at the bottom of the page for you to use.

By the way, the email they send you will look authentic because they send it from an email spoofing site, and so it will say something like Joe.blo@xyzbank.com. Totally believable. When you click on that link, they will even make the URL that appears at the top of your screen in the address bar. But in the background, the browser is pointed to the hacker's server When you get there you will see your page to enter your user id and pass word. That happens after this is not important because at this point, the hacker now has your username and password and he can log in whenever he wants.

This kind of social engineering is sophisticated and is used often for more than just theft. In many cases, the unsuspecting user becomes party to a money laundering scheme. Once the hackers know they have your account information, they pass it to the Dealer who then sets up the con. In money laundering operations, money is transferred to your account without you knowing and then transferred out. It's not until the Feds show up that you know anything has happened. It becomes even more sinister if the hacker had used your computer using a RAT to log into your bank account and to conduct the transfers.

There will be no way for you to prove to the Feds that it wasn't you.

Torrents

Torrents are popular places to get infected. Most people don't even realize it until it's too late. The moment you click on the link at your torrent app kicks in, part of the virus is already on its way in. Within the file is an executable portion that gets in and writes itself into the registry or gets into the hard drive and thereafter into the startup sequence. This is a persistent virus. In many cases, the AV programs do not detect them. One trick that most antiviruses, including Virustotal, do not scan for is a file that is sufficiently compressed. When a file is compressed, it changes the signatures that the AV algorithm is programmed to search for. So when the file is uploaded and your AV software scans it, it won't be detected. Some antivirus software can detect them but the one that none of them seem to be able to get over is when the hacker breaks the program apart and then uses an assembly script to pull the different parts and assemble the program after it has been scanned. Writing such a script is fairly easy and anyone with Python or C experience can whip a program like that up in less than 20 minutes. Because the torrents that come in are in large files and come from different locations, the program that is downloaded is a small script that gets the computer to find a specific URL and download the file autonomously. So this will happen, for instance when the computer is left unattended, and the screensavers are running, this program will begin is download in the parts and the assembly and then the execution. This kind of infections does not need to be socially engineered, they can be sent out in large quantities and infect large groups of people. Sometimes the same computer can be infected multiple times.

DDOS Threats

We wrote earlier about bots that could be bought, sold and rented to people who wanted to use them for an array of activities. One of those activities is to conduct DDOS attacks. A DDOS attack is a Distributed Denial of Service attack. It just means that the mastermind takes all the bots at his disposal and attacks one website. Or server. When all the requests for web pages hit the server in close succession or on top of each other, the server gets overwhelmed and has to shut down.

These kinds of attacks tend to cause a lot of trouble for companies that manage websites and for the companies that on the sites. It has come to a point where the companies just pay the ransom as soon as the threat of DDOS is mentioned. That is the power of this tool. The hackers just need to get everything ready and ask for the ransom. Without even touching one button, the hackers make away with their ransom. This is called DDOS Ransom and the payments are typically made via Bitcoin. All the while the DDOS is going on, the owners of the computers that are taking part in the attack have no idea that their computer had been hijacked and that it is part of an attack. In fact, once it has started, the owner might feel a little reduction in performance but nothing serious

Chapter 4 The Vulnerabilities of the System

The best way to become a hacker is to get some programming skills and thereafter create your own bot net. This is hypothetical and you shouldn't really do it because it is illegal in most countries. But even though hacking activity is illegal, it is hard to prove and it is even harder to convict unless the enforcement agency, typically the FBI, has been monitoring you over a period of time and is building a case against you that they give you enough rope to hang yourself. Some of the major hackers, both Consumers, and Dealers, have been monitored closely and patiently before traps were sprung on them.

The trick to understanding hackers is to imagine yourself as being one and that's how the rest of the books is going to be phrased. There is an old aphorism – "Think like a thief, to catch a thief." And so to proceed through the rest of the book, we will pretend to be thieves so that you can understand and think like they do.

The Hackers Five Commandments

1. Computers are targets, data is the prize – people don't exist. IN other words, it's all just bits of data. Nothing personal.
2. Code is God. Everything you can do, you can do with code.
3. The stronger the firewall, and the more complex the AV, the more you have to try. It's a challenge.
4. If the system is weak, the owner deserves to be hacked.
5. All systems can be breached.

If you are to be a hacker the one rule of the five that you must always remember is that between the system and the user, there is always a vulnerability that can be exploited until you have full control of the machine. The only way that you cannot control the machine is if you can't find the machine in the first place.

IP Addresses and NMAP

The first weakness that is in the infrastructure of the Internet is that each computer comes with its own unique IP number and IMAC number. The IP number is assigned by the router and the Router is assigned the IP number by the ISP. So you have a forward facing and rear facing IP. Your computer's IP is usually in the 192 range. Your router, on the other hand, would have an IP based on your country and state.

Even though I do not know you or your computer, as long as I can scan your network and find that there is a live computer at the end of the IP address, I can get to work. Remember NMAP. Well, all I have to do is scan that network and I will have your IP address and your IMAC number.

The way to get around this is to do one of two things. First, get yourself a paid subscription to a VPN. VPN stands for Virtual Private Network. If a computer is behind a VPN, they won't even show up on a NMAP scan. How could someone hack you if you are invisible? Hackers love VPNs so that they can use it to remain anonymous, but hate the fact that target computers can use it too because it makes targets invisible.

The ability to map IP numbers is inherent in the system and it is one of the major weaknesses that can be exploited. The next weakness is the operating system itself. There are numerous operating systems out here and the most popular by far is the MS Windows based system. At the time of this writing, the most recent Windows is Windows 10. It is one of the most stable of all the windows even though it is still new but it is doing well. However, no matter how well it does, it is still an MS based system and the system comes with a few kinks in it that always lend itself to getting hacked.

OS Vulnerabilities and Metasploit

There are so many vulnerabilities that can be uncovered that it would be almost impossible for any single human being to know all the possible variations and weaknesses to exploit. That's why there is a software that can do it for you.

This software that you definitely need if you are to ever become a credible hacker or pen tester is called Metasploit. Not many outside the industry know this. It is a fantastic tool backed up by a dynamic and vibrant community. The community continuously backs up the system with any vulnerabilities it finds and the company behind the software keeps the systems up to date. So when you find a system using NMAP, you turn on Metasploit and you check to see if the system has any vulnerabilities that you can use.

Once you find the vulnerability then you can choose from any one of a number of tools within the Metasploit framework to exploit that vulnerability. You could inject the system to shut it down, or you could inject the system with a RAT and take control. Many times hackers just create a persistent back door and leave it as it is. SO that when they sell the penetrated computer to the Dealer, the dealer can just walk into the back door and do whatever he wants to.

The tips I am giving you here will allow you to become a hacker almost overnight. But that is not why I am doing that. I am showing you how easy it is to become a hacker and how much hackers tend to make that it should worry you enough to take sufficient measures to keep your computer and your data safe. Don't say I didn't warn you.

Wi-Fi Vulnerabilities and Interception

I mentioned this a little earlier. There is such a thing called the Man in The Middle Attack, or MITM. You've already gotten to know about this and I've also mentioned Wireshark – the software that lets you peek into anyone's traffic.

But there are a number of other things that you should consider. The first is to safeguard your Wi-Fi router. If you don't there are consequences that will make you wish you did.

The first for a hacker who wants to gain access to your home system is to sit outside your house on the curb. Perhaps in his car at night when no one is watching and scan for all the Wi-Fi signals in the neighborhood. From the curb, where you would probably get few signals, you could choose your target easily. All he has to do is use one of the available WIFI Cracking software on the market (again, it's free) the one that works quite well for WEP passwords is Aircrack. When you use this software, the script goes in and resets the system and that automatically triggers the Wi-Fi to query the users for user id and password. When the occupant of the home signs back in, he broadcasts his user id and password in a way that Aircrack can capture it. The only thing left to do is crack the encryption which is not too difficult. There are numerous websites that have databases for that purpose. It typically takes about 30 minutes to get into a Wi-Fi network without a password.

The other easy way of doing it is to just look at the NMAP scan and find out the name of the WIFI router. Then do an online search for that model's default username and password. You should be able to get it easily. Once you have the Wi-Fi password, you can log in and access the internet from the at Wi-Fi hotspot. But more than just grabbing someone's internet access, what you also have now is the ability to use Wireshark to tap into their network and snoop on the traffic that passes back and forth. From there you will be able to grasp all the information you need. It is also possible to inject a virus or an access tool that will make its way onto the home computer and from there be able to turn the desktop into a bot.

Phishing

Phishing is such an old strategy but it remains a powerful and effective one because people keep falling for it. The point here is never to click on links. If you have to find the website and navigate there yourself. It should be a rule that you never breach because, as you have seen, hackers can take you to any site as soon as you click on it even if it says that it is supposed to take you to a site that you are familiar with. Never sign in to your accounts after following a link. Banks and credit card companies will never (NEVER) send you emails and ask you to click on a link to your account and ask for password and user id credentials.

SQL Mapping

So far we have focused on hacks that happen downstream. But even if you protect yourself to the fullest extent, there Is away that hackers can still get to you. The idea is to inject viruses into popular websites. Some time ago, I had 42 websites that were all ranking number one on Google. Business was good. Within a month of getting to the top spot, I started noticing certain glitches in my site but didn't think anything of it. Then I started getting complaints from visitors who came to the site. Apparently, their AV had detected virus on the site and within a week after that Google removed all of them from their indexing and my pages couldn't be found anywhere on the search engine results. It cost me a lot of money but taught me a powerful lesson. Apparently what had happened was that these hackers monitored sites that are turning in the top half of the Google SERPs. They then head to the site and try to penetrate it. If successful, they inject a virus into the site so that when visitors clicked on a link they got infected. The way they did it was simple. They started by getting a bunch of keywords from Google and ran the search. They then go to a list of websites in the SERPs and then used an SQL mapping tool to find out if there are vulnerabilities in the SQL database. If there is, then all they had to do was exploit it and they would be able to enter the website's admin area and insert whatever they wanted into the page without much notice.

This is called SQL injection. And to do it there are tools like SQL MAP or SQL Ninja that can do this.

These are a number of other ways to gain access to other so as to find financial data or personal data or just snoop around and convert the computer to a bot. I've presented this in a way that looks like you can be the hacker, but as I've said repeatedly it is to show you how easy it is and there are kids below the age of 12 that can do this without much effort.

Chapter 5 Why Antiviruses Don't Really Work

While it is very important that you have a strong AV on your system and that you keep it updated and active, it is not a total defense to your system. The best way is to stay anonymous on the web and for that, you should get a paid VPN service. Something like hidemyass.com. They are one of the few that have been in the market for quite some time.

Most people think that they can just get a run of the mill AV and not even pay for it by getting a free copy off the net and hope that it will protect them. It won't. It's not about whether the copy is free or paid for, it's about the fact that the AV – Virus game is like the cat and mouse Olympics. Each one is trying to get one up on the other. But the game is rigged in such a way that the virus always gets the upper hand because there are always vulnerabilities to exploit and it takes time for the software programmers to catch up and fix it.

When you see a virus scan that has caught a virus, I am sure you feel like it was worth the effort in purchasing and installing the AV. But the problem does not stop there. The virus that the AV blocked probably belonged to some unsophisticated newbie hacker. The real hackers who probably already have control of your computer know exactly what will and what won't fly in the face of the latest AV updates. They are not in the game to try and fail. These are highly motivated and highly liquid players that jack your computer for a specific reason and that reason is so much more than you can imagine until you read this book.

I am not asking you to go out and delete your AV protection. No, don't do that because then instead of just being controlled by the smart hackers, you will also be slaved to the stupid ones. To be able to stay off the hacker's surveillance, as I've said you need to get off the grid. You need to use the VPN and disappear. That's the first step. The second step requires that you get good surfing habits.

It would be ridiculous to say that you should be very careful where you land, but within reason, you should stay away from sites that I mentioned earlier. You should stay away from sites that offer free porn, free torrents, illegal software and anything in that vein. But the thing that is most important about getting the VPN is that even if a hacker were to be able to get a

RAT on to your system if you are behind a VPN, that RAT would not be able to connect back to the master.

Along these lines, you should also get a tool to monitor your outbound traffic. The tool that you can purchase will sit in your tray and in the event any program requests for an outbound connection, you will be alerted. So, in the event you get a RAT installed by accident, you will hear about it the first time it tries to 'phone home'.

Chapter 6 Chances are You are Already Hacked

If you have been online on your computer and you have a certain habit of surfing, and if you have opened links that have been forwarded to you by friends, then there is a better than 90% chance that you have been infected by some form of virus, and also a chance that you have been infected by a dormant virus that has created a back door for some Dealer to come in at a point later when he has the need. Even when he does come in and use it, you probably wouldn't know about it, unless it was something that was really egregious that the authorities have been monitoring. And pin the crime on you.

The only way to not be hacked is to stay off the Internet, but that would make no sense. So what you have to do is follow the advice in the last chapter. For now what you need to do is protect your computer and your data, especially your financial documents.

The first thing you should do is get a thumb drive that holds your private files and secret passwords in an encrypted file and keeps that out of the computer until you need to use it. Once you finish using it, then you need to unplug and put it away.

Change your passwords weekly and do not use words. There are databases of commonly used words that hackers have access to that can do a brute force attack and if you are using a simple password, they will have it cracked in less than an hour. To keep your data safe, use a phrase or a sentence. For instance instead of using solar system as your password, make it ilovedaisieinthespring (it reads, I love daisies in the spring) then convert some of the alphabets to numbers. I take all the o's and make it zeros. So it will look like this ilovedaisiesinthespring. But that's still not enough. Change all the i's to 1. So now you have something like this 1loveda1s1es1nthespr1ng you can then separate the words with * so now you have 1*love*da1s1es*1n*the*spr1ng. This makes the password almost impossible to guess and so a brute force attack would be impossible. You could then mix it up some more and add capital letters to the mix and so on.

The other thing that you should do is keep these passwords in a folder that you encrypt. When you need to enter the passwords into the site, cut and paste them so that in case there is a keystroke logger in your system, then they would not be able to record the keystrokes and get your password from there.

You also must make sure that your email passwords and your bank passwords are never the same. In fact, none of your secure sites should share the same passwords. Don't use your personal email as your banking email contact and make sure you use two step authentication whenever it is offered.

Btu right now let's assume you are already hacked. What you need to do is get all the passwords to your online sites changes. You should keep a handwritten log of all the sites. Inventory all your sites, usernames and passwords and keep them somewhere safe. Don't forget to change the most important ones weekly (especially if they do not have 2-step authentication).

Chapter 7 How to Prevent Cyber Theft

In a best case scenario, hackers will get away with some cash through fraud, but in a worst case scenario they can wreck your credit and cause you to lose your home and your job by ruining your credit without your knowledge. The best way to fix this is to never trust public networks. You can leave public networks out of your diet by never getting on them, or having a special device that carries none of your personal info so that even if it is infiltrated hackers won't get anything. I have three devices at any one time. There is my phone which is purely for communication and never gets on a Wi-Fi network, private or public. That means my contact list is safe and even if my friends' are not as careful and they inadvertently give up my number when they are hacked, the hacker is only going to be able to get my phone number but won't be able to get anything else.

My second device is a laptop that does not use WIFI but uses mobile broadband. It's a little more expensive but it's safer. All my data is stored in the cloud with accounts that require two-step authentication. The second step authentication needs code verification using my phone. Finally, the third device is a desktop that uses fixed line internet and is connected to a VPS, a virtual private server. If anyone hacks my router or my desktop they would first have to deal with my firewall that is set too high. Then they could have to try to sniff my data that is streaming in and out of my device but that is encrypted. So all they are going to get is a stream of gibberish.

My passwords are not simple words or dates but instead, they are composed of long sentences or phrases which I change every week. Trying to brute force my password would take a super computer more than a hundred years to crack. My hard drive at home has zero data on it. And all my important data is kept off the grid.

I also have a network monitor that reports to me what program is trying to gain access to the internet. If it's suspicious I kill it.

Conclusion

So what have we learned? Well, it's the wild west out there. You need to accept that fact and you need to prepare for that. Your financial data is probably the most valuable thing that hackers are looking for aside from your IP address to use in a DDOS attack.

Experts are already predicting a trillion dollar expenditure for anti-cybercrime efforts over the next five years. It's easy to get desensitized with all these big numbers flying around. But don't be complacent. Those are big numbers and when the numbers are that big and growing, there will be no reason to stop. So you can be sure that hacking and cybercrime is here to stay. The penalties are already harsh in most jurisdictions, but that does not seem to halt or slow it down.

There are also new comers to this world of hacking because of the intrigue and the profit potential. I am sure some of you may even think about it after reading this book. My sincere advice is don't do it. If you find it to be a lot of fun that you would like to play around with it, I suggest you do two things. One, you set up an old computer as a server or as a computer and try to hack that, or you go to one of those sites that are designed for penetration testing. For a fee, they will allow you to hack them and see how far you get. But more importantly, you should play around with it so that you can get a grasp of what hackers do so that you can protect yourself and your data better.

The main target of these hackers are to either steel assets and convert that to money, or to launder the ill-gotten funds, this includes fraudulent transactions and withdrawals In the money laundering process.

Cybercrime is a wide area and can include many areas, only a few include hacking and fraud that flows from the hacking. Nonetheless, it is still a big business that can cost innocent victims more than 300 billion dollars annually. The ability to hack a system is not difficult to learn and it can be lucrative. The last time someone sent out a ransom ware virus, he made a way with a tidy sum. It wouldn't make them totally wealthy so that they could retire, but it does paint a bleak picture. Cybercrime, especially hacking, is set to expand and the methods are set to become more sophisticated. Just fifteen years ago, hackers needed to know the computers inside and out. They needed to be experts at coding and needed to know their way around the network and the operating system. They were specialists and they were knowledgeable in what they did. All that has changed today. You can download any software you need in the guise of pen-testing, and you would have a range of actions that are all automated. You could mix and match the tools to get different outcomes and you could successfully social engineer campaigns that harvested thousands of botnets at a time. You could then pull data from their finances and the party would just be getting started.

All this paints a bleak picture and while you shouldn't' worry about the rest of the world, you should only concern yourself with how you are going to protect your computer and your information.